Girl Please, Do You!

Stop Shrinking, Start Shining—How to Set Boundaries and Own Your Space

Lola Devine

© **Copyright 2024 - All rights reserved.**

The content contained within this book may not be reproduced, duplicated or transmitted without direct written permission from the author or the publisher.

Under no circumstances will any blame or legal responsibility be held against the publisher, or author, for any damages, reparation, or monetary loss due to the information contained within this book, either directly or indirectly.

Legal Notice:

This book is copyright protected. It is only for personal use. You cannot amend, distribute, sell, use, quote or paraphrase any part, or the content within this book, without the consent of the author or publisher.

Disclaimer Notice:

Please note the information contained within this document is for educational and entertainment purposes only. All effort has been executed to present accurate, up to date, reliable, complete information. No warranties of any kind are declared or implied. Readers acknowledge that the author is not engaged in the rendering of legal, financial, medical or professional advice. The content within this book has been derived from various sources. Please consult a licensed professional before attempting any techniques outlined in this book.

By reading this document, the reader agrees that under no circumstances is the author responsible for any losses, direct or indirect, that are incurred as a result of the use of the information contained within this document, including, but not limited to, errors, omissions, or inaccuracies.

Table of Contents

Introduction: Girl, It's Time to Stop Shrinking and Start Shining	1
Why Women Shrink Themselves	2
Boundaries: The Magic Word You Didn't Know You Needed	3
Why Doing You is the Ultimate Power Move	4
What You'll Discover in this Book	5
Let's Get Started	6
Chapter 1: Relationships – Loving Without Losing Yourself	7
Practical Tips and Strategies	10
Where Do You Stand?	12
What Your Answers Say About You	12
Chapter 2: Family Ties – The Fine Line Between Support and Sacrifice	14
Practical Tips and Strategies	16
Family's Rock or Standing Tall?	19
Your Takeaway	20
Chapter 3: Career – Working Hard Without Being Worked Over	21
Practical Tips and Strategies	23
Boss Babe or Work Mule?	26
What This Means for You	27
Chapter 4: Money – Earning, Spending, and Investing in Yourself	28
Practical Tips and Strategies	30
Financially Fabulous or Fiscally Fearful?	33
How You're Doing	34
Chapter 5: Body & Health – Prioritizing Self-Care Without Guilt	35
Practical Tips and Strategies	37
Self-Care Queen or Self-Care Crisis?	40
Your Scorecard	41
Chapter 6: Social Expectations – Saying No to Society's Shoulds	42

Practical Tips and Strategies	44
Authentically You or Society's Puppet?	47
The Breakdown	48
Chapter 7: Fear – Conquering the Boundaries of Self-Doubt	**49**
Practical Tips and Strategies	51
Fearless Queen or Fear's BFF?	53
What's the Verdict?	54
Chapter 8: Friendship – Being a Supportive Friend Without Being a Doormat	**55**
Practical Tips and Strategies	57
Bestie or Doormat?	59
Your Reflection	60
Chapter 9: Time – Guarding Your Calendar and Your Sanity	**61**
Practical Tips and Strategies	63
Time Boss or Overcommitted Queen?	66
How You Measure Up	66
Chapter 10: Identity – Reclaiming Who You Are at Every Stage of Life	**68**
Practical Tips and Strategies	70
True to You or Playing a Role?	72
The Big Reveal	73
Conclusion: Girl, You've Got This!	**74**
Key Takeaways from Girl Please, Do You!	75
Keep Applying These Lessons to Your Life	78
Embrace the Journey	79
Girl, Keep Shining!	79

Introduction: Girl, It's Time to Stop Shrinking and Start Shining

> "You owe it to yourself to stop apologizing for who you are and start living boldly for who you want to be."

Girl, stop right there. Yes, YOU. Before you even think about sacrificing your sanity to make someone else happy, let's have a little heart-to-heart. How many times have you put yourself on the back burner because someone else needed you to come through? Be honest. How many times have you said yes when everything in you was screaming no? You've been doing it for years—shrinking to fit in, dimming your light so others can shine, making yourself smaller so no one feels uncomfortable around you. But let me tell you something: it's time to stop. It's time to reclaim what's yours—your space, your dreams, your voice, your power.

And that's what this book is all about. *Girl Please, Do You!* is your permission slip to stop shrinking and start shining. This is the guide you didn't know you needed to set boundaries, own your space, and unapologetically *do you*. And trust me, this isn't about being selfish or cold-hearted—this is about being real. It's about standing tall in who you are, what you want, and what you deserve.

If you're tired of being pulled in a thousand directions, if you're ready to stop bending over backward for everyone but yourself, and if you're craving more out of life—then girl, this is the place for you.

Why Women Shrink Themselves

Let's get real for a second. Society has been telling women for ages that we need to be everything for everybody—supportive, nurturing, self-sacrificing, and basically the glue that holds it all together. Whether it's relationships, family, or career, we've been sold this idea that our worth comes from how much we can give, how many people we can please, and how little space we take up. Sound familiar?

We've all heard the subtle (and sometimes not-so-subtle) messages:

- "Be a good wife, a good mother, a good daughter."
- "Don't be too loud. Don't be too bold."
- "Put others before yourself."
- "Sacrifice your needs for the greater good."

Girl, I'm here to tell you that it's time to throw those old tapes out. Women have been shrinking themselves for way too long—emotionally, mentally, and even physically. We're constantly bending, folding, and twisting ourselves to fit into boxes that don't even make sense. We sacrifice our desires, our goals, our well-being for the sake of others, and most of the time, it's done without a second thought. But at what cost?

When was the last time you actually took a moment to ask yourself:

- "What do *I* want?"
- "How am *I* feeling?"
- "Am I living the life *I* dreamed of?"

Too often, the answer is, "I don't know" or worse, "I can't remember." But here's the truth: when you shrink yourself, you're not doing anyone any favors. In fact, you're robbing the world of the full, vibrant, badass version of YOU. And honey, the world needs you to show up as *all* of yourself, not just the pieces that make others comfortable.

Boundaries: The Magic Word You Didn't Know You Needed

Let's talk about boundaries—because if there's one thing that will change your life, it's learning how to set them. Boundaries are the difference between thriving and barely surviving. They're the invisible lines that tell the world, "This is who I am, this is what I need, and this is how I deserve to be treated." But here's the kicker: you have to set them. No one is going to do it for you.

Why? Because boundaries make people uncomfortable, especially when they're used to you bending over backward to accommodate their needs. But girl, let me tell you: boundaries are *not* about keeping people out; they're about letting the right people in—those who respect your space, your time, and your energy. Boundaries are about creating a life where you are in control, where you get to say what works for you and what doesn't.

But I get it—setting boundaries isn't always easy. We've been taught to feel guilty for saying no, to feel bad for putting ourselves first. We worry that if we set boundaries, people will think we're rude, selfish, or worse, that they'll leave us. But here's the thing: if someone can't respect your boundaries, they're not meant to be in your life. Period. End of story.

Setting boundaries is like planting a flag in your own personal space. It's declaring, "I am important, my needs matter, and I won't compromise my well-being for anyone." And guess what? When you start setting boundaries, you'll realize that the right people—the people who truly value and respect you—will stick around. They'll appreciate you even more for knowing your worth.

Why Doing You is the Ultimate Power Move

This book is about more than just boundaries; it's about living life on your own terms. It's about reclaiming your power and stepping into the fullest, most authentic version of yourself. Because girl, here's the deal: when you do you, everyone wins.

Think about it—when you're living authentically, when you're taking care of yourself, when you're clear about what you need, you're happier, healthier, and more fulfilled. And when you're thriving, you have so much more to give to the people around you. It's like the oxygen mask on an airplane—you have to secure your own mask before helping anyone else. The same goes for life. You can't pour from an empty cup, and you can't give what you don't have. So, it's time to fill up your cup, girl, and let it overflow.

This book will walk you through the areas of life where women tend to shrink themselves the most—relationships, family, career, money, body image, social expectations, and more. In each chapter, we'll dig deep into why these areas are so tricky, how society sets us up to shrink, and most importantly, how to stop. You'll learn practical tools to start setting boundaries, reclaiming your space, and saying "yes" to yourself without guilt. And at the end of each chapter, you'll take a little quiz to see if you're truly doing you or if you've still got some shrinking to undo.

What You'll Discover in this Book

So, what's the journey ahead, you ask? Here's a sneak peek of what you'll discover in each chapter:

- **Relationships:** How to love and be loved without losing yourself.
- **Family:** The fine art of balancing support and self-preservation.
- **Career:** How to thrive at work without being worked over.
- **Money:** Earning, spending, and investing in YOU.
- **Body & Health:** Making self-care a priority, not an afterthought.

- **Social Expectations:** Breaking free from society's shoulds and living life your way.
- **Fear:** How to conquer self-doubt and step boldly into your dreams.
- **Friendship:** Being there for your friends without being their emotional doormat.
- **Time:** Guarding your calendar like the precious resource it is.
- **Identity:** Reclaiming who you are, no matter the roles you play.

Each chapter will give you the tools to recognize where you've been shrinking, practical steps to stop, and a fun, sassy quiz to help you assess your progress. By the end of this book, you'll not only be setting boundaries like a pro, but you'll also be living your life unapologetically, authentically, and most importantly—joyfully.

Let's Get Started

So, are you ready to stop shrinking and start shining? Are you ready to set boundaries, own your space, and do you? If so, grab your favorite pen (and maybe a glass of wine), settle in, and let's get to work. This journey is about reclaiming your power and stepping into the life you were meant to live. It won't always be easy, but I promise it will be worth it. And along the way, I'll be here cheering you on—because girl, if anyone deserves to shine, it's you.

This is your moment. This is your life. And it's time to do YOU.

Chapter 1: Relationships – Loving Without Losing Yourself

"Love should expand who you are, not erase you. The strongest relationships are built on mutual respect, not self-sacrifice."

Let's talk about relationships—those beautiful, messy, complicated, and sometimes all-consuming connections we form with other people. Whether it's with a partner, a friend, or a family member, relationships have this incredible way of making us feel seen, loved, and understood. But, girl, they also have a sneaky way of making us disappear.

It starts small—maybe you compromise a little more than you wanted to, or you let something slide that you would've normally stood up for. Suddenly, you're agreeing to plans you don't even like, nodding along to ideas that don't feel right, and bending over backward to make sure the other person is happy, even if it means sacrificing your own happiness.

Sound familiar? You're not alone. Women are often conditioned to believe that their worth in relationships comes from how much they give, how flexible they are, and how well they can cater to others' needs. We're taught that being "low maintenance" is a badge of honor, that being agreeable makes us lovable, and that putting our own desires first somehow makes us selfish.

But here's the thing, sis: a relationship is supposed to lift you up, not shrink you down. You should be able to love someone fully without losing yourself in the process. The problem arises when we start to give too much of ourselves—when we become so focused on keeping the peace, making others happy, or being the "perfect" partner that we forget who we are and what we need.

Healthy love doesn't ask you to sacrifice your identity. It doesn't require you to silence your voice, abandon your dreams, or pretend to be someone you're not. Healthy love celebrates who you are in all your messy, magical glory. But for that to happen, you need boundaries. You need the courage to say, "This is who I am, and I'm not going to change that to make you more comfortable."

In this chapter, we're going to dive deep into how relationships can cause us to shrink, and most importantly, how to stop. It's time to reclaim your voice, your needs, and your space in relationships—whether it's with your partner, your best friend, or even your mom. Let's start with a little story that might feel all too familiar.

Meet Chloe. Chloe is the textbook example of "the giver" in relationships. She's the girl who's always there for her partner, the one who rearranges her entire life to make sure her boyfriend has everything he needs. Sounds sweet, right? But here's the catch—Chloe has forgotten what *she* needs. Her boyfriend, Tom, is a decent guy, but he's become so used to Chloe bending over backward that he doesn't even think to ask what she wants anymore.

Take last weekend, for example. Chloe hates camping. The bugs, the dirt, the lack of showers—no, thank you. But when Tom casually mentioned that he wanted to go camping with his friends, she plastered on a smile and said, "Sure, sounds fun!" By the time they were sitting around a smoky campfire with her swatting at mosquitoes, she was silently screaming, "Girl, what am I doing here?"

But it's not just camping. Chloe finds herself saying yes to everything Tom wants, from his favorite restaurants to his weekend plans. Meanwhile, her desires—the spa day she's been craving, the art class she wanted to sign up for—are pushed further and further down the list.

At this point, Chloe is more a reflection of Tom's interests than her own. And while Tom is living his best life, Chloe is slowly fading into the background. It's not that Tom doesn't love Chloe—he does. But Chloe has trained him to believe that she'll go along with anything. And the sad part? She thinks this is what makes her a good partner.

Practical Tips and Strategies

Girl, it's time to snap out of the "people-pleaser" fog. Loving someone doesn't mean you lose yourself. If you're constantly compromising, giving in, or silencing your wants to maintain the peace or keep someone happy, you're not in a healthy relationship —you're in a one-sided one. Here's how to reclaim your space and set the boundaries you need to thrive in love:

1. **Know Your Non-Negotiables**
   Before you can set boundaries in a relationship, you need to know what your non-negotiables are. What are the things you absolutely need in a relationship to feel happy, secure, and fulfilled? Maybe it's having regular "me time," maybe it's making sure your partner respects your career goals, or maybe it's simply being able to express your feelings without judgment. Write down your non-negotiables and own them. These aren't things you're willing to sacrifice—not for anyone.

2. **Communicate Your Needs Early and Often**
   One of the biggest mistakes we make in relationships is assuming our partners know what we need. Girl, let me tell you —no one is a mind reader. If you're constantly expecting your partner to just "get it," you're setting yourself up for disappointment. Start communicating your needs early in the relationship, and don't stop. If you need time to yourself, say it. If you want more emotional support, ask for it. Clear communication is the foundation of healthy boundaries.

3. **Stop Saying Yes When You Mean No**
   Chloe's mistake wasn't that she hated camping—it was that she said yes to something she didn't want to do. If you find yourself agreeing to things that don't feel right or that you simply don't enjoy, it's time to start saying no. You don't have to be rude

about it, but you *do* have to be firm. Saying no doesn't mean you don't care about the other person—it means you care about yourself enough to honor your feelings.

4. **Practice Self-Care, Guilt-Free**
   Self-care isn't selfish—it's essential. Make time for the things that bring you joy, whether it's a hobby, a spa day, or simply reading a book in peace. And when you take that time for yourself, do it without guilt. Remember, you're not just a partner—you're a whole person with needs and desires that deserve to be nurtured.

5. **Address Imbalance with Love, Not Frustration**
   If you've been in a relationship where you've constantly bent over backward, it can be hard to suddenly start setting boundaries. But girl, you've got to start somewhere. Sit down with your partner and have an honest conversation about the imbalance in the relationship. Instead of coming from a place of frustration or blame, approach the conversation with love. Let them know that you're making changes because you want the relationship to thrive—and that means you need to feel seen and heard too.

Stick to Your Boundaries, Even When It's Hard

Setting boundaries is one thing—sticking to them is another. There will be times when your partner (or friends, or family) push back against your boundaries. They might not like the new you, the one who says no, who prioritizes her needs, who doesn't cater to their every whim. But girl, this is your time to shine. Hold firm. Boundaries are there for a reason, and if someone can't respect them, it's time to reevaluate the relationship.

Where Do You Stand?

Are you owning your individuality in love, or have you been losing yourself along the way? Let's find out—take this quick check-in and see how you're doing!

1. When your partner suggests plans that you don't really enjoy, do you:
   - A. Politely suggest an alternative that makes you both happy.
   - B. Agree to go along with it, even though it's not your thing.
3. How often do you find yourself giving in just to avoid conflict?
   - A. Rarely—I speak up when something doesn't feel right.
   - B. Often—I'd rather just keep the peace.
5. Do you have regular "me time" that's just for you, even when in a relationship?
   - A. Absolutely! My personal time is non-negotiable.
   - B. Not really. My partner's needs usually come first.
7. When was the last time you said no to something you didn't want to do in your relationship?
   - A. Recently—I'm learning to prioritize my feelings.
   - B. Can't remember—I usually just go with the flow.

What Your Answers Say About You

- **Mostly A's:** *Girl, you're doing YOU!* You know how to love without losing yourself, and you've got those boundaries locked in. Keep shining!

- **Mostly B's:** *Girl, it's time to reclaim your space.* You've been shrinking in your relationship, and it's time to start speaking up for what you need. Set those boundaries and do you!

Chapter 2: Family Ties – The Fine Line Between Support and Sacrifice

> "Family ties should support you, not bind you. True connection comes from love and respect, not losing yourself in obligation."

Family—where would we be without them? They're the people who know us best, who've been there since day one, and who will likely be around for most of our lives. But here's the thing about family: they can be just as demanding as they are loving. Whether it's your parents, siblings, or even extended relatives, the expectations that come with family relationships can be overwhelming. You want to be there for them, help when needed, and make them proud—but sometimes, in trying to do all that, you end up sacrificing yourself in the process.

Maybe it's constantly saying yes to their requests, even when you're already stretched thin. Maybe it's feeling guilty for setting boundaries with family members because, well, "they're family." Or maybe it's trying to live up to their expectations, even when those expectations don't align with your own dreams and goals.

The truth is, we're often taught that family comes first—no matter what. But here's the twist: putting family first shouldn't mean putting yourself last. Loving your family doesn't have to come at the expense of your mental health, your happiness, or your personal growth. And setting boundaries with family isn't about shutting them out—it's about protecting your energy and well-being while still being able to show up for them in a healthy way.

In this chapter, we're going to talk about the fine line between being supportive and being sacrificial. We'll explore how to set boundaries with family (even the guilt-tripping ones), how to balance your needs with theirs, and how to love your family without losing yourself in the process.

Because, girl, if you're not careful, you can end up being the family's go-to person for everything—from hosting holiday dinners to fixing everyone's problems—until you're left with nothing for yourself. It's time to learn how to say no, how to prioritize yourself, and how to reclaim your space while still being the loving, thoughtful daughter/sister/niece/aunt that you are.

Let's meet Brianna. Brianna is the "fixer" in her family. You know the type—she's the one everyone calls when things go wrong. Her brother needs help moving? Brianna's got it. Her parents need someone to organize the family reunion? Of course, it's Brianna. Cousin Tina's kids need a last-minute babysitter? Call Brianna.

But here's the problem: Brianna is exhausted. She's so busy taking care of her family that she barely has time to take care of herself. She hasn't had a Saturday to herself in months because she's always running from one family emergency to the next. And the worst part? She feels guilty every time she thinks about saying no.

The other day, her mom asked her to host yet another holiday dinner. Brianna sighed and agreed, even though she'd promised herself she'd take a break this year. As she was prepping her third pie at midnight, she muttered to herself, "Girl, what have you gotten yourself into?"

It's not that Brianna doesn't love her family—she does. But somewhere along the way, she forgot that loving them doesn't mean being at their beck and call 24/7. And now, Brianna feels like she's drowning in family obligations, with no time or energy left for herself.

Practical Tips and Strategies

Girl, if you're feeling like Brianna—constantly overwhelmed by family responsibilities—it's time to make some changes. Here's how to start setting boundaries with your family and reclaim your time, energy, and sanity:

1. **Get Clear on Your Priorities**
   The first step to setting boundaries with family is figuring out what your own priorities are. What's most important to you

right now? Is it your career? Your health? Your hobbies? Your relationships outside of the family? You can't set boundaries if you don't know what you're protecting. Take some time to reflect on what matters most to you and how much time and energy you want to devote to family obligations versus your personal goals. Once you're clear on your priorities, you'll be able to set boundaries that align with them.

2. **Learn the Art of Saying No (Without the Guilt)**
   This one's tough, but it's essential. Saying no to family doesn't mean you love them any less—it just means you're honoring your own needs. The next time a family member asks for something that you don't have the time or energy for, practice saying no with love. You can say something like, "I'd love to help, but I've got a lot on my plate right now. I hope you understand." Trust me, they'll survive without you swooping in to save the day. And here's the kicker: the more you practice saying no, the easier it gets.

3. **Set Clear Expectations**
   Sometimes family members don't even realize they're overstepping your boundaries because you've always been so accommodating. It's time to reset those expectations. Have a heart-to-heart with your family and let them know what you're available for and what you're not. For example, you might say, "I'm happy to help out occasionally, but I won't be able to take on any more regular responsibilities." Be firm, but compassionate, and don't be afraid to stick to your boundaries.

4. **Let Go of Guilt**
   Family can be great at guilt-tripping, whether they mean to or not. You might hear things like, "But we're family! You have to help!" or "I thought you'd always be there for us." But girl, here's the truth: you can love your family without being their

doormat. Feeling guilty for prioritizing your own well-being is a trap. Remember, taking care of yourself isn't selfish—it's necessary. You can't be there for others if you're constantly running on empty. Let go of the guilt and embrace the freedom that comes with setting healthy boundaries.

5. **Delegate, Delegate, Delegate**

   Just because you're good at something doesn't mean you have to do it all the time. If your family has come to rely on you for certain things—like hosting dinners, organizing events, or managing family affairs—start delegating. Pass the torch to someone else. You don't have to carry the entire load on your shoulders. Trust that your family can step up and take responsibility, and if they don't, that's on them—not you.

6. **Take Time for You**

   This one's non-negotiable. You need time for yourself, away from family obligations. Whether it's scheduling regular "me time" on the weekends, going on a solo vacation, or simply setting aside an hour each day to do something you love, make sure you're carving out space for yourself. This time is sacred, and it's essential for your mental and emotional well-being.

7. **Address Resentment Before It Builds**

   If you find yourself feeling resentful toward your family for always needing something from you, that's a sign that your boundaries have been crossed. Don't wait until you're burned out and ready to explode—address those feelings early on. Let your family know when you're feeling overwhelmed and communicate your needs clearly. It's better to have a tough conversation now than to let resentment fester and damage your relationships in the long run.

Family's Rock or Standing Tall?

Curious if you've been giving too much to family or if you've mastered the art of setting boundaries? Let's find out—take this quiz to see how you're doing!

1. When your family asks you to host the holiday dinner (again), do you:
    - A. Gently suggest that someone else take over this year.
    - B. Say yes, even though you really don't want to.
3. How often do you feel like you're the one everyone turns to for help?
    - A. Rarely—I've set clear boundaries with my family.
    - B. All the time—I'm the family's go-to person for everything.
5. Do you have regular time set aside just for you, away from family obligations?
    - A. Absolutely! My personal time is a priority.
    - B. Not really—I'm too busy helping everyone else.
7. When a family member tries to guilt-trip you into helping, do you:
    - A. Stick to your boundaries and politely decline.
    - B. Give in because, well, they're family.

Your Takeaway

- **Mostly A's:** *Girl, you're doing YOU!* You've got those family boundaries on lock, and you know how to love your family without losing yourself. Keep shining!

- **Mostly B's:** *Girl, it's time to reclaim your space.* You've been sacrificing too much for family, and it's time to start setting some boundaries. Remember, you can love your family *and* take care of yourself.

Chapter 3: Career – Working Hard Without Being Worked Over

"Money is a tool, not a measure of your worth. True wealth comes from using it to build a life that reflects your values and dreams."

Now let's talk about the place where many of us spend most of our time: the workplace. The career grind can be thrilling, rewarding, and—let's be honest—exhausting. Whether you're chasing the next promotion, trying to prove your worth, or just trying to keep your head above water, it's easy to get caught in the trap of overworking, over-pleasing, and undervaluing yourself.

In the professional world, women are often expected to wear multiple hats while smiling through it all. We're told to be team players, to lean in, to go above and beyond. And, girl, don't get me started on the "good girl" syndrome that tells us to be agreeable, to never rock the boat, and to just keep the peace—even when it's at the expense of our own career satisfaction.

But here's the hard truth: no one's going to give you the recognition you deserve if you keep shrinking yourself. Staying late, saying yes to every extra task, volunteering for projects that no one else wants—these things might make you feel like you're being helpful, but what they're really doing is telling your colleagues and boss that you're okay with being taken advantage of. And sis, you deserve more than that.

It's time to stop being the office workhorse and start being the boss of your own career. And that doesn't necessarily mean you need to quit your job or change industries (unless you want to, of course). What it means is that you need to start setting clear boundaries in the workplace, advocating for yourself, and demanding what you deserve. Because guess what? You're not just a cog in the machine—you're a powerhouse who has every right to claim her spot at the table.

In this chapter, we're going to dive deep into the dynamics of the workplace and how women often shrink themselves for the sake of keeping the peace or appearing "easygoing." We'll cover how to set boundaries with your boss and colleagues, how to advocate for your worth, and how to take control of your career trajectory—without burning out or losing yourself along the way.

Meet Janae. Janae is what you might call a "people pleaser" in the workplace. She's the one who says yes to everything, no matter how full her plate is. Need someone to cover a shift? Call Janae. Got an extra project that no one wants to take on? Janae's your girl. Late-night meetings? Of course, Janae will be there with coffee and a smile.

But while Janae is bending over backward to make sure everyone else is happy, she's silently drowning in work. She's staying late every night, working weekends, and losing sleep over deadlines that don't even belong to her. Her boss praises her for being a "team player," but when it comes time for promotions or raises, Janae is mysteriously overlooked.

One Friday evening, after canceling yet another dinner with friends to stay late for a project that wasn't even hers, Janae had a moment of clarity. As she stared at her computer screen, exhausted and frustrated, she thought, "Girl, what are you doing? You're running yourself ragged for a job that isn't giving you what you deserve."

That's when Janae realized she had been shrinking herself in the workplace for far too long. She was so focused on being helpful and accommodating that she forgot to advocate for her own needs and goals. And girl, once she had that realization, there was no going back.

Practical Tips and Strategies

If you're feeling like Janae—overworked, underappreciated, and stuck in the people-pleasing cycle—it's time to flip the script and start advocating for yourself. Here's how to set boundaries and reclaim your space in the workplace:

1. **Stop Saying Yes to Everything**

    The first step to reclaiming your power at work is learning how to say no. This doesn't mean you're shirking responsibilities—it means you're protecting your time and energy. When your boss or colleagues come to you with extra tasks, ask yourself if this is something that aligns with your career goals or if it's just busywork. If it's the latter, politely decline or delegate. You can say something like, "I'd love to help, but my plate is full right now. Let's see if we can find someone else to take this on."

2. **Set Clear Boundaries with Your Time**

    One of the biggest mistakes we make in the workplace is allowing our work to bleed into our personal lives. If you're staying late, answering emails after hours, or sacrificing your weekends for work that could wait until Monday, it's time to set some boundaries. Let your boss and colleagues know that your time outside of work is important, and you won't be available 24/7. A simple "I'll take care of this first thing tomorrow" can do wonders for reclaiming your time and sanity.

3. **Know Your Worth and Advocate for It**

    If you're constantly over-delivering but not seeing the rewards (whether that's a raise, a promotion, or even just recognition), it's time to advocate for yourself. Don't wait for your boss to magically notice your hard work—schedule a meeting and lay out your contributions. Be clear about what you want, whether it's a raise, a promotion, or more challenging projects. It might feel uncomfortable at first, but girl, no one is going to fight for your worth if you don't.

4. **Delegate When Possible**

   Just because you *can* do something doesn't mean you *should* do it all. If you're in a position where you can delegate tasks, do it. This frees up your time to focus on higher-level work and prevents you from getting bogged down in menial tasks that don't move the needle on your career. And if you're not in a position to delegate yet, start advocating for more help or resources to lighten your load.

5. **Create a Work-Life Balance Non-Negotiable List**

   Write down the things that are non-negotiable for you when it comes to work-life balance. Whether that's leaving the office by 6 p.m., not checking work emails on the weekends, or taking a full lunch break every day, these are the boundaries you need to protect your well-being. Communicate these non-negotiables with your boss and team, and stick to them—even when it's tempting to "just do a little more."

6. **Recognize Burnout and Address It Head-On**

   Burnout doesn't happen overnight—it creeps up on you slowly, as you take on more and more until you're overwhelmed. If you're feeling exhausted, detached from your work, or resentful of your job, it's a sign that burnout is on the horizon. Don't wait until you hit rock bottom to address it. Start setting boundaries now to prevent burnout, and if you're already feeling burned out, take time off to recharge and reassess your priorities.

7. **Stand Tall and Don't Shrink Yourself for Others' Comfort**

   This is a big one. In many workplaces, women are taught to be "team players," to be agreeable, and to not make waves. But girl, shrinking yourself to make others comfortable will only keep you stuck. Stand tall in your abilities, your worth, and your goals. Speak up in meetings, share your ideas, and don't let imposter syndrome convince you that you're not good enough. You are more than capable, and it's time to start owning it.

Boss Babe or Work Mule?

Curious to see if you've been running the show in your career or if you've been running yourself into the ground? Take this quiz to find out!

1. When your boss asks if you can take on yet another project, do you:
   - A. Politely decline and suggest a timeline that works better for you.
   - B. Say yes and then scramble to figure out how to fit it in.
3. How often do you check work emails or take calls after hours?
   - A. Rarely—I set clear boundaries for my time outside of work.
   - B. Often—I feel like I have to stay connected to keep up.
5. When was the last time you advocated for a raise or promotion?
   - A. Recently—I regularly discuss my career goals with my boss.
   - B. I can't remember—I don't want to rock the boat.
7. Do you feel like your workload is manageable, or are you constantly overwhelmed?
   - A. Manageable—I've set boundaries and delegate when needed.

- B. Overwhelmed—I'm always buried under tasks.

What This Means for You

- **Mostly A's:** *Girl, you're doing YOU!* You've got your work boundaries in check, and you're advocating for yourself like the boss babe you are. Keep climbing that career ladder on your terms!
- **Mostly B's:** *Girl, it's time to reclaim your space.* You've been shrinking yourself at work, and it's time to start setting some boundaries. Remember, you deserve to thrive in your career, not just survive it.

Chapter 4: Money – Earning, Spending, and Investing in Yourself

> "Health is the foundation of everything you do—invest in it unapologetically, because your well-being is your greatest strength."

Let's talk about money. Ah yes, that magical thing that makes the world go round—or at least keeps the bills paid, right? Money is one of those topics that can be exciting, stressful, empowering, and intimidating all at the same time. And let's be real—when it comes to money, many of us women have been conditioned to think that we should be responsible with it, but not necessarily *bold* about it.

We're told to save for a rainy day, to be frugal, to make sure we're taking care of others, and to not take too many risks. Sound familiar?

But here's the problem: for a lot of women, managing money is tied up with guilt. Guilt about spending money on ourselves. Guilt about earning more than others. Guilt about wanting financial independence. And, girl, don't even get me started on how we've been taught to put other people's financial needs before our own—whether it's family, a partner, or even friends.

The truth is, money is power. And when you shrink yourself financially—whether that's under-earning, over-giving, or avoiding investment in yourself—you're giving away your power. You deserve to earn what you're worth, to spend without guilt, and to invest in the things that make you thrive—whether it's a business, a dream, or even just your own well-being.

In this chapter, we're going to talk about how to stop shrinking when it comes to money. We'll cover how to get comfortable with earning, how to set financial boundaries (yes, they exist!), and how to stop feeling guilty about spending on yourself. It's time to start thinking about money as a tool for empowerment, not a source of shame. Because girl, you're worth every penny—and then some.

Meet Sabrina. Sabrina is great at saving. She has a solid emergency fund, she's paid off her credit cards, and she's always the one her family turns to when they need financial advice. But here's the thing—Sabrina never spends any money on *herself*. Like, ever.

Last month, Sabrina got a bonus at work—$2,000 that she wasn't expecting. Instead of treating herself to something nice (because

Lord knows she deserves it), she immediately thought about how she could help her little brother with his car payment or how she could add it to her family's vacation fund. When her best friend suggested she use some of it to book a weekend at a spa, Sabrina brushed it off, saying, "I can't justify spending that kind of money on myself."

Fast forward to last week, and Sabrina is still working long hours, feeling exhausted, and thinking, "I need a break." But she hasn't spent a dime of that bonus on herself. Why? Because she's been taught that money is for practical things, for saving, for giving to others—not for her own pleasure or well-being.

As Sabrina sat at her kitchen table, staring at her tired reflection in the window, she muttered, "Girl, why are you so afraid to spend money on *you*?"

That's when it hit her: it wasn't about the money. It was about feeling like she didn't deserve to invest in herself. But girl, you deserve it. Every woman does.

Practical Tips and Strategies

If you've ever felt like Sabrina—hesitant to spend money on yourself or unsure of how to set financial boundaries—it's time to shift your mindset and reclaim your financial power. Here's how to start earning, spending, and investing in *you* without guilt:

1. **Know Your Worth and Stop Under-Earning**
   One of the biggest ways women shrink financially is by under-earning—whether that's taking jobs that don't pay enough, not negotiating for higher salaries, or undervaluing your skills in the marketplace. Girl, it's time to stop accepting less than what

you're worth. If you know you're being underpaid, it's time to have a conversation with your boss about a raise. If you're freelancing or running your own business, raise your rates. You deserve to be compensated fairly for your time and expertise.

2. **Set Financial Boundaries with Family and Friends**
It's common to feel obligated to help family or friends financially, especially if you're in a more stable financial position than they are. But here's the truth: you can't pour from an empty cup. It's important to set boundaries around how much you're willing to give—whether it's a loan, a gift, or just covering a bill. You can help without sacrificing your own financial security. The next time someone asks for money, don't be afraid to say, "I'm not in a position to help right now." You don't need to justify it beyond that.

3. **Spend on Yourself Without Guilt**
Spending money on yourself isn't selfish—it's self-care. Whether it's a massage, a new outfit, or a weekend getaway, you deserve to enjoy the money you've worked so hard to earn. Create a "fun money" budget that's just for you, and commit to spending it every month. That might mean buying something small each week or saving up for a bigger treat—but whatever it is, do it without guilt. You're not just paying bills and helping others—you're also investing in your own happiness.

4. **Start Thinking About Money as a Tool for Empowerment**
Instead of viewing money as something to hoard or something to fear, start thinking about it as a tool for empowerment. What dreams have you put on the back burner because of money? Maybe you've always wanted to start your own business, go back to school, or take a life-changing trip. Use your money to invest in the things that bring you closer to your goals. Don't be

afraid to take risks with your money, especially when it's an investment in yourself.

5. **Create a Financial Plan that Includes *You***

    When you're creating a budget or financial plan, it's easy to focus on the "shoulds"—you should save more, you should invest, you should pay off debt. But girl, where are *you* in that plan? Make sure your financial plan includes money for things that bring you joy. That might mean setting aside money for a personal hobby, taking a class you've always wanted to, or even just treating yourself to a nice dinner every now and then. You work hard, and you deserve to enjoy the fruits of your labor.

6. **Talk About Money Openly**

    One of the reasons women often shrink financially is because we're not taught to talk about money openly. Whether it's salary negotiation, managing debt, or investing, money conversations are often taboo. But girl, you need to start talking about money—especially with other women. The more we share, the more we empower each other to make smart financial decisions. Talk to your friends about how much you're earning, ask for advice on investing, or share your money goals. The more transparent you are, the more confident you'll feel about managing your money.

7. **Plan for the Future, but Live in the Present**

    It's important to save for the future, but don't let that stop you from living in the present. Yes, have an emergency fund. Yes, contribute to your retirement. But don't forget to enjoy your life *now*. Money is meant to be spent—not just saved. So while you're being smart about your financial future, make sure you're also using your money to create a life you love today.

Financially Fabulous or Fiscally Fearful?

Wondering if you've got your money game on point or if you're still shrinking when it comes to finances? Take this quiz and find out!

1. When you get a bonus at work, do you:
    - A. Treat yourself to something special—you've earned it!
    - B. Save it all or use it to help someone else.
3. How comfortable are you talking about money with friends or colleagues?
    - A. Very comfortable—I believe in being transparent about money.
    - B. Not comfortable at all—money conversations make me nervous.
5. Do you have a "fun money" budget that's just for spending on yourself?
    - A. Absolutely! I make sure to budget for the things I love.
    - B. Not really—I feel guilty spending money on myself.
7. How often do you say no to financial requests from family or friends?
    - A. Often—I've set clear financial boundaries.
    - B. Rarely—I feel obligated to help, even if it stretches me thin.

How You're Doing

- **Mostly A's:** *Girl, you're doing YOU!* You've got your money game on lock, and you're not afraid to earn, spend, and invest in yourself. Keep shining and building that financial empire!

- **Mostly B's:** *Girl, it's time to reclaim your financial space.* You've been shrinking when it comes to money, and it's time to start setting some boundaries. Remember, you deserve to enjoy your money just as much as anyone else!

Chapter 5: Body & Health – Prioritizing Self-Care Without Guilt

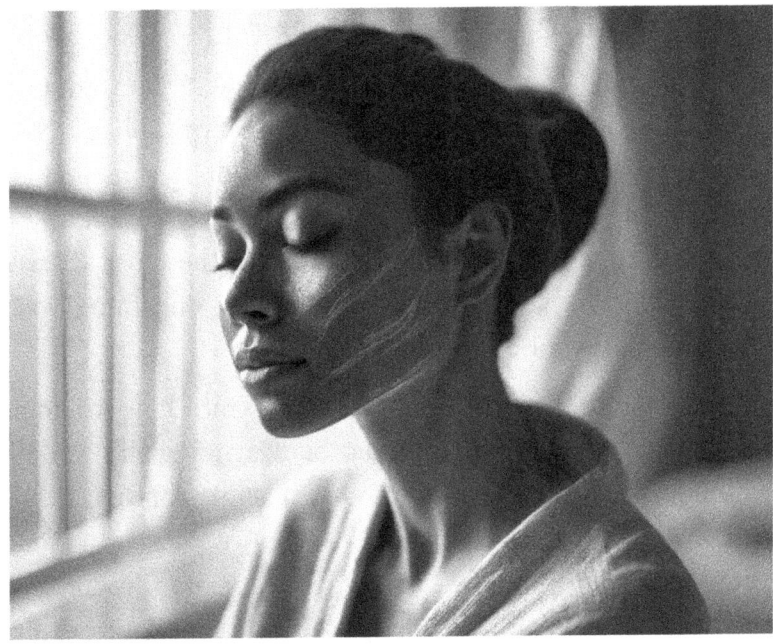

> "Harmony in health is about finding balance—nurturing your body, mind, and soul to thrive, not just survive."

Let's get real, girl—how many times have you skipped that workout, canceled that spa day, or ignored your body's cries for rest because something "more important" came up? We've all been there. Whether it's taking care of the family, staying late at work, or juggling a million things on your to-do list, self-care is usually the first thing to get kicked to the curb. Why? Because we've been taught that our health and well-being come *after* we've taken care of everyone and everything else. It's like self-care is this luxurious treat we have to "earn" by completing our long list of duties. Spoiler alert: that's a load of nonsense.

Here's the truth: your health—physical, emotional, and mental—is *not* something you should put on the back burner. It's not optional. You can't keep pouring from an empty cup, and if you keep ignoring your body, it's going to let you know. (And trust me, you don't want to wait for that wake-up call.)

But, girl, I get it. We live in a world where "hustle culture" is glorified, where being constantly busy is worn like a badge of honor, and where taking time for yourself is somehow seen as selfish. But let me tell you something—there's nothing selfish about prioritizing your health. In fact, it's the most selfless thing you can do. Because when you're running on fumes, you're not showing up as your best self for anyone.

In this chapter, we're going to dive deep into how women shrink themselves when it comes to their bodies and health—whether it's skipping that doctor's appointment, pushing through exhaustion, or constantly putting others' needs before your own well-being. And more importantly, we'll talk about how to flip the script and start making self-care a *priority* without guilt. Because, girl, your health isn't negotiable.

Meet Jessica. Jessica is the queen of "I'll take care of myself later." She's always on the go—working long hours, taking care of her kids, volunteering at her community center, and somehow still managing to keep her house spotless. But with all that going on, guess who she forgets to take care of? Yep, herself.

Last month, Jessica started feeling run down. She had been waking up with headaches, her back was constantly sore, and she couldn't remember the last time she got a full night's sleep. But instead of slowing down, she just kept pushing through. She'd tell herself, "I'll take a break next week," but of course, next week would come and go, and she'd still be running on empty.

Then one day, while running late to yet another meeting, Jessica's body had had enough. She felt dizzy, nauseous, and had to sit down before she passed out. That was her body screaming, "Girl, what are you doing?!"

As she sat there, trying to catch her breath, she realized she had been treating self-care like a luxury instead of the necessity it is. "Girl," she thought to herself, "it's time to start taking care of *you*."

Practical Tips and Strategies

If you've ever felt like Jessica—constantly putting others' needs before your own and running on fumes—then it's time to make a change. Here's how to start prioritizing your health and self-care without feeling guilty:

1. **Stop Waiting for "The Perfect Time" to Take Care of Yourself**
   There's no such thing as the perfect time to start taking care of yourself. Life will always be busy, and there will always be something that seems more urgent. The key is to stop waiting for a break and start *creating* time for self-care. Schedule that workout, book that massage, take that afternoon off—do

whatever it takes to prioritize your well-being. Treat it like any other appointment, and don't cancel on yourself.

2. **Listen to Your Body—It Knows What It Needs**
Your body is always sending you signals, whether it's that little nagging ache, the constant fatigue, or the stress headache that just won't quit. But here's the problem: we're so used to pushing through the discomfort that we ignore the signals until they're screaming at us. Start tuning in to your body's needs, and respond to them. If you're tired, rest. If you're in pain, address it. If you're feeling anxious or overwhelmed, take a break. Your body knows what it needs, and it's your job to listen.

3. **Make Self-Care a Non-Negotiable**
Self-care isn't a reward for when you've "earned it." It's a necessity. If you don't make time to take care of yourself, your body will eventually force you to slow down—whether through illness, burnout, or exhaustion. Start treating self-care like a non-negotiable part of your routine. That might mean carving out time every day for exercise, meditation, or just sitting quietly with a cup of tea. Whatever it is, make it a priority, and don't let anything (or anyone) take that time away from you.

4. **Set Boundaries Around Your Time and Energy**
One of the biggest reasons women neglect their health is because they're constantly giving their time and energy to others. Whether it's work, family, or friends, it's easy to let other people's needs take precedence over your own. But girl, it's time to start setting some boundaries. Protect your time and energy like your life depends on it—because it does. That means saying no to things that drain you, delegating tasks when possible, and making sure you have time carved out for rest and relaxation.

5. **Get Comfortable with Rest**

   Rest isn't a luxury—it's a vital part of maintaining your health. But so many of us feel guilty when we rest, like we should be doing something more productive. Girl, let me tell you: rest *is* productive. It's when your body repairs itself, when your mind gets to recharge, and when you regain the energy to tackle the world. So stop feeling guilty for taking a nap, for sitting on the couch with a good book, or for simply doing *nothing* for an afternoon. You need it.

6. **Don't Be Afraid to Ask for Help**

   A lot of women think they have to do it all—work, family, social life—and they feel like asking for help is a sign of weakness. But girl, that couldn't be further from the truth. Asking for help is a sign of strength. Whether it's delegating tasks at work, asking your partner to take on more responsibilities at home, or hiring a babysitter so you can have some time to yourself, asking for help allows you to focus on your well-being. Don't be afraid to lean on others.

7. **Treat Your Health as an Investment, Not an Expense**

   Whether it's paying for a gym membership, buying healthy groceries, or seeing a therapist, it's easy to view spending money on your health as an unnecessary expense. But girl, your health is the best investment you can make. When you're healthy, you have more energy, more focus, and more ability to show up in all areas of your life. So instead of feeling guilty about spending money on your well-being, start seeing it as an investment in your future.

Self-Care Queen or Self-Care Crisis?

Ready to find out if you've been prioritizing your health and self-care or if you've been putting yourself last? Take this quiz and see where you stand!

1. When you feel run down or exhausted, do you:
    - A. Take a break, rest, and listen to your body.
    - B. Push through and tell yourself you'll rest later.
3. How often do you cancel or reschedule self-care appointments (like the gym, a massage, or a doctor's visit)?
    - A. Rarely—my self-care appointments are non-negotiable.
    - B. Often—I always feel like something more important comes up.
5. Do you feel guilty when you take time for yourself to relax or rest?
    - A. Not at all—rest is a part of my self-care routine.
    - B. Yes, I always feel like I should be doing something productive.
7. How often do you set boundaries around your time and energy to protect your well-being?
    - A. Often—I've learned to protect my time and energy.
    - B. Rarely—I find it hard to say no to others.

Your Scorecard

- **Mostly A's:** *Girl, you're doing YOU!* You've made self-care and health a priority, and it shows. Keep listening to your body and setting those boundaries—you're on the right track!

- **Mostly B's:** *Girl, it's time to reclaim your health.* You've been putting yourself last for too long, and it's time to start prioritizing your well-being. Remember, you can't pour from an empty cup, and your health is non-negotiable.

Chapter 6: Social Expectations – Saying No to Society's Shoulds

> "True friendship lifts you up, not weighs you down. Set boundaries that let you give and receive with grace."

Let's talk about the "shoulds" in life—you know, all those things society tells you you *should* do. You should be polite. You should dress a certain way. You should settle down by a certain age, have a certain job, and basically live according to a pre-approved checklist. The problem? Those "shoulds" can keep you stuck, small, and shrinking in places you don't even realize. And girl, who wants to live life according to someone else's rules?

The expectations placed on women can be relentless. Whether it's the way you look, act, or live, there's always some societal voice whispering in your ear, telling you that you're not measuring up. You're too loud, too opinionated, too independent—or maybe you're not ambitious enough, not skinny enough, not *enough* in some way. These standards aren't just unattainable—they're exhausting.

It's time to stop letting society's "shoulds" dictate how you live your life. Here's the truth: you don't owe anyone your conformity. You don't need to follow the crowd, meet arbitrary expectations, or live up to outdated standards of what a woman "should" be. You only need to be true to *yourself* —and that starts by recognizing where these pressures come from and learning to say "no" to them.

In this chapter, we're going to unpack some of the biggest social expectations women face and how they can shrink us if we're not careful. More importantly, we'll talk about how to stand tall, push back against those "shoulds," and start living a life that's authentically yours. Because girl, the only thing you *should* be is unapologetically you.

Meet Olivia. Olivia has always been the "good girl." She did everything she was supposed to—got good grades, went to college, landed a stable job, and settled into a "respectable" career. On paper, Olivia's life looked perfect. But deep down? She was miserable.

See, Olivia had always dreamed of becoming an artist. But that wasn't part of the plan. When she told people about her dreams, she was met with responses like, "That's not practical" or "You should stick to a real job." So, she shelved her passion and followed the "shoulds" instead. She put on the blazer, went to the office, and lived a life that looked great from the outside—but left her feeling empty.

One day, after yet another day of staring at spreadsheets and wondering what the point was, Olivia had a realization. "Girl, who are you living for?" she asked herself. She was checking off all the boxes, but none of them were *her* boxes. Olivia decided right then that she was done living by society's rules. It was time to take the path that felt right to her—even if it didn't make sense to anyone else.

Practical Tips and Strategies

If you've ever felt like Olivia—stuck in a life that's been dictated by what others think you *should* do—it's time to break free. Here's how to start pushing back against social expectations and reclaim your right to live on your terms:

1. **Identify the "Shoulds" in Your Life**
   The first step to breaking free from societal expectations is recognizing where they're showing up in your life. Take some time to reflect on the "shoulds" that have been guiding your decisions. Do you feel pressure to look a certain way, have a certain job, or follow a specific life path? Write down all the expectations you've internalized, and then ask yourself: *Whose expectations are these?* Often, you'll find that the things you've been striving for aren't even your own desires—they're society's, your family's, or your peers'. And girl, that's the first sign it's time to let them go.

2. **Challenge the Unspoken Rules**

    Once you've identified the "shoulds" that have been guiding you, it's time to start challenging them. Why do you believe you have to fit into a certain mold? Who benefits from you playing by these unspoken rules? (Hint: it's probably not you.) Start questioning why these rules exist in the first place and whether they actually serve you. The more you challenge these expectations, the more you'll realize that most of them are arbitrary and don't align with who you truly are.

3. **Define Success on Your Own Terms**

    Society has a pretty narrow definition of success—one that often revolves around money, status, and outward appearances. But girl, success doesn't have to look like what everyone else says it should. Take some time to define what success means to *you* . Maybe it's building a creative career, traveling the world, or simply finding peace and balance in your everyday life. Whatever it is, make sure it's a definition that lights you up—not one that's been handed to you by someone else.

4. **Stop Seeking External Validation**

    One of the biggest reasons we get caught up in societal expectations is because we're constantly seeking approval from others. We want people to like us, to accept us, to think we're doing well. But here's the truth: the more you seek external validation, the more you'll find yourself living a life that's not your own. It's time to stop caring so much about what others think and start caring about what *you* think. The next time you make a decision, ask yourself: *Is this what I want, or am I doing it to impress someone else?*

5. **Create Boundaries Around Your Choices**

    When you start living authentically, not everyone is going to understand. Some people might question your choices, try to give you unsolicited advice, or even guilt-trip you into staying on the "traditional" path. But girl, that's where boundaries come in. Create firm boundaries around your choices and stick to them. You don't owe anyone an explanation for how you choose to live your life. You can simply say, "I've made my decision, and I'm happy with it." Period. End of discussion.

6. **Embrace Your Uniqueness**

    One of the most powerful things you can do is embrace your uniqueness and let go of the need to fit in. You weren't put on this earth to be like everyone else—you were made to stand out. So, stop shrinking yourself to meet society's standards and start celebrating the things that make you different. Whether it's your style, your interests, or your life path, embrace it all. Because girl, life is too short to spend it trying to be someone else.

7. **Surround Yourself with People Who Support You**

    It's a lot easier to live authentically when you're surrounded by people who lift you up, support your choices, and encourage you to be yourself. Seek out relationships with people who celebrate your uniqueness and respect your boundaries. Let go of the ones who try to box you in or make you feel like you need to fit a certain mold. The people who truly care about you will love you for who you are—not for who they think you *should* be.

Authentically You or Society's Puppet?

Curious to know if you're living life on your terms or if you're still letting society's "shoulds" guide you? Take this quiz to find out!

1. When you make a major life decision (career, relationships, etc.), do you:
    - A. Make the decision based on what feels right to *you* .
    - B. Worry about what others will think or expect.
3. How often do you find yourself trying to fit into a specific mold or standard?
    - A. Rarely—I live life according to my own rules.
    - B. Often—I feel pressure to meet certain expectations.
5. Do you seek approval from others before making personal choices?
    - A. No—I trust my own judgment and don't need external validation.
    - B. Yes—I like to get others' opinions before making big decisions.
7. How comfortable are you with standing out or being different from the crowd?
    - A. Very comfortable—I embrace my uniqueness.
    - B. Not very comfortable—I prefer to fit in and follow the crowd.

The Breakdown

- **Mostly A's:** *Girl, you're doing YOU!* You're living life authentically and on your own terms. Keep embracing your uniqueness and saying no to society's "shoulds." You've got this!

- **Mostly B's:** *Girl, it's time to reclaim your space.* You've been letting society's expectations dictate your life for too long. It's time to start living for *you* and pushing back against the "shoulds." Remember, you don't owe anyone conformity.

Chapter 7: Fear – Conquering the Boundaries of Self-Doubt

"Fear may whisper doubts, but courage speaks louder. Step forward boldly, even when the path feels uncertain."

Let's talk about fear. And no, I'm not talking about the "scared of spiders" kind of fear. I'm talking about that quiet, sneaky, creeping fear that whispers in your ear: *"What if I'm not good enough? What if I fail? What if people don't like me?"* The kind of fear that holds you back from chasing your dreams, speaking your mind, or taking that leap of faith.

Fear shows up in different ways for different women, but one thing is for sure: it's a powerful force. It can paralyze you, keep you small, and convince you that you're better off staying in your comfort zone, even if that comfort zone is holding you back. Fear often masquerades as practicality, as safety, as "playing it smart." But girl, let's call it what it really is—it's self-doubt, and it's shrinking you.

Here's the thing about fear: it's not going away. It's always going to be there, in one form or another. But the key isn't to get rid of fear—it's to learn how to live with it, and more importantly, how to move forward *despite* it. The most courageous people aren't fearless—they're the ones who feel the fear and do it anyway.

In this chapter, we're going to dig into how fear shows up in your life, how it keeps you from being your most authentic self, and how to conquer it. Whether it's fear of failure, fear of judgment, or fear of stepping outside the box, it's time to reclaim your power. Because girl, the life you're dreaming of is waiting for you on the other side of fear.

Let me tell you about Maya. Maya had always wanted to start her own business. She had a passion for design, a sharp business mind, and an idea that could really take off. But every time she thought about quitting her corporate job to pursue her dream, fear swooped in like an uninvited guest at the party.

"What if it fails?"
"What if no one likes my designs?"
"What if I'm not cut out for this?"

These were the questions that kept Maya stuck at her 9-to-5, even though every day at her desk felt like she was slowly suffocating. She would sit there, daydreaming about her business, but the moment she thought about taking the leap, fear tightened its grip. So, she stayed. Safe. Comfortable. But unfulfilled.

One night, after another long day at work, Maya sat in her car and asked herself, "Girl, what are you so afraid of?" The truth? She was more afraid of *never* trying than she was of failing. And that's when it hit her: if she didn't take the leap, she'd never know what could've been.

So, she took a deep breath, handed in her resignation, and went all-in on her dream. Was she still scared? Absolutely. But she realized that fear wasn't a reason to stop—it was just part of the journey.

Practical Tips and Strategies

If you've ever felt like Maya—wanting to move forward but feeling paralyzed by fear—it's time to push past that self-doubt and start taking control. Here's how to start facing your fears and moving forward with courage:

1. **Acknowledge the Fear (But Don't Let It Take Over)**
   The first step to conquering fear is acknowledging that it exists. Don't try to ignore it or push it down. Instead, name it. Say it out loud: "I'm afraid of failing," or "I'm afraid of being judged." Acknowledging your fear takes away some of its power. Once you've named it, you can start to work with it, rather than letting it control you.

2. **Ask Yourself: What's the Worst That Could Happen?**
   One of the most effective ways to deal with fear is to confront it head-on. Ask yourself, "What's the worst that could happen if I

fail?" Often, when you play out the worst-case scenario, you realize that it's not nearly as bad as you've been imagining. Failure isn't the end of the world—it's a stepping stone to success. And guess what? You're resilient enough to handle whatever comes your way.

3. **Flip the Script: What's the Best That Could Happen?**
While we're busy worrying about the worst, we often forget to imagine the best. What if you succeed beyond your wildest dreams? What if people *love* your ideas? What if taking that leap opens doors you never even knew existed? Instead of focusing solely on the risks, start thinking about the potential rewards. Fear often tricks us into only seeing the downside—so it's up to you to remind yourself of the upside.

4. **Take Small, Courageous Steps**
You don't have to tackle your biggest fears all at once. Sometimes, all it takes is a small, courageous step to build momentum. Maybe it's speaking up in a meeting when you'd usually stay quiet. Maybe it's submitting your work to that competition you've been eyeing. Or maybe it's simply sending that email you've been putting off because you're nervous about the response. Each small step chips away at the fear, building your confidence along the way.

5. **Reframe Failure as a Learning Experience**
One of the biggest reasons we fear failure is because we see it as a reflection of our worth. But girl, failure is not the opposite of success—it's part of the journey. Every successful person has failed at something; the difference is that they didn't let failure stop them. Start seeing failure as feedback, as an opportunity to learn and grow. The more you reframe failure, the less intimidating it becomes.

6. **Surround Yourself with People Who Believe in You**

   Fear thrives in isolation, so one of the best ways to combat it is to surround yourself with a support system that believes in you. Whether it's friends, family, or a mentor, having people who lift you up can make all the difference when fear tries to pull you down. Share your fears with someone you trust, and let them remind you of your strengths and capabilities.

7. **Develop a Fear-Busting Mantra**

   When fear starts creeping in, it can help to have a mantra that snaps you out of it. Something simple, yet powerful, like "I am brave enough," or "I can handle this." Repeat it to yourself whenever fear rears its head. Mantras are a way to ground yourself in the present moment and remind yourself that you're stronger than the fear you're facing.

8. **Remember: Fear is Normal (and Temporary)**

   Here's a little secret: everyone feels fear. Even the people who seem the most confident, the most successful—they feel fear too. The difference is, they've learned not to let it stop them. Fear is a normal part of life, but it doesn't last forever. Once you take action, the fear starts to fade, and in its place, you'll find strength, courage, and the realization that you can handle more than you think.

Fearless Queen or Fear's BFF?

Wondering if fear is running the show in your life, or if you're taking control? Take this quiz and find out!

1. When you're faced with a big opportunity, do you:
    - A. Go for it, knowing that fear is part of the process.

- B. Hesitate and second-guess yourself until the opportunity passes.

3. How often do you hold back from speaking your mind because you're afraid of being judged?
    - A. Rarely—I speak up when I have something to say.
    - B. Often—I worry about what others will think.

5. When you think about failure, do you:
    - A. See it as part of the journey and a chance to learn.
    - B. See it as something to avoid at all costs.

7. Do you take small steps toward your goals, even when you're scared?
    - A. Yes—I'm learning to act despite fear.
    - B. Not really—I tend to let fear stop me before I even begin.

What's the Verdict?

- **Mostly A's:** *Girl, you're doing YOU!* You're learning to feel the fear and do it anyway. Keep taking those courageous steps —you're on your way to greatness!
- **Mostly B's:** *Girl, it's time to reclaim your power.* Fear has been keeping you stuck for too long. Start taking small steps toward your goals, and remember—you're stronger than you think!

Chapter 8: Friendship – Being a Supportive Friend Without Being a Doormat

"Time is your most valuable currency—spend it wisely on what fuels your soul, not just what fills your schedule."

Let's talk about friendship—one of the most beautiful and enriching parts of life. Good friends lift us up, make us laugh, and support us through thick and thin. But girl, let's be honest: friendships can also be complicated. While you want to be there for your friends, it's easy to slip into a pattern where you're giving more than you're receiving, where you're the one always showing up, doing the emotional labor, and putting your own needs aside to make sure everyone else is okay.

Friendship should be a two-way street. But too often, women find themselves stuck in friendships where they're constantly overextending themselves, afraid to set boundaries, and feeling drained instead of uplifted. Maybe you have that one friend who always needs you, but never really checks in on how you're doing. Or maybe you're the one everyone calls when there's a crisis, but when you need a shoulder to lean on, it's crickets. Sound familiar?

Here's the deal: being a good friend doesn't mean being a doormat. You can be supportive, loving, and present without sacrificing your own well-being. It's time to stop shrinking yourself in your friendships, girl. You deserve to have friendships that are balanced, that fill you up instead of draining you, and where you feel valued—not just for what you can give, but for who you are.

In this chapter, we're going to talk about how to set boundaries in friendships, how to be supportive without losing yourself, and how to recognize when it's time to let go of a friendship that's no longer serving you. Because real friendship is about mutual respect, care, and understanding—not about one person always giving while the other takes.

Meet Keisha. Keisha is the go-to friend in her circle. Whenever someone has a problem, they call Keisha. Need advice? Call Keisha. Going through a breakup? Call Keisha. Want to rant about a bad day at work? You guessed it—call Keisha.

Now, don't get me wrong—Keisha loves being there for her friends. She's the supportive, dependable type. But over time, something started to feel off. Every time Keisha had a problem or needed to vent, it seemed like no one had time for her. She started to realize that while she was always showing up for her friends, they weren't really showing up for her in the same way.

One day, after spending three hours on the phone comforting a friend who was upset over yet another relationship drama, Keisha hung up and thought, "Girl, when was the last time anyone listened to *your* problems?" That's when it hit her—her friendships were out of balance. She was giving and giving, but her friends weren't reciprocating. And Keisha knew that something had to change.

Practical Tips and Strategies

If you've ever felt like Keisha—constantly being the supportive friend but rarely getting the same in return—it's time to reset the balance in your friendships. Here's how to start setting boundaries, reclaiming your energy, and building more reciprocal, healthy friendships:

1. **Recognize When the Friendship Is Out of Balance**
   The first step in addressing imbalanced friendships is recognizing when you're giving more than you're receiving. Take a moment to reflect on your current friendships. Are you always the one reaching out, listening, and providing support? Do you feel like your needs are being met, or are you constantly putting yourself on the back burner for others? Identifying the imbalance is the first step to creating healthier relationships.

2. **Communicate Your Needs Clearly**
   It's easy to assume that friends know what we need, but here's

the thing—no one is a mind reader. If you're feeling like your friendships are one-sided, it's time to speak up. Let your friends know when you need support, too. It can be as simple as saying, "I've been going through a tough time, and I could really use someone to talk to." If your friends value you, they'll step up. If they don't? Well, that tells you everything you need to know.

3. **Set Boundaries Around Emotional Labor**
   Emotional labor is the invisible work of being the "therapist" friend—the one who listens to everyone's problems, offers advice, and takes on the emotional weight of others. While it's important to be supportive, you don't have to be your friends' unpaid therapist. Set boundaries around how much emotional labor you're willing to take on. If a friend constantly calls you to vent without ever asking how you're doing, it's okay to say, "I love you, but I'm feeling a bit overwhelmed right now. Can we talk about something lighter?"

4. **Evaluate Whether the Friendship Is Truly Reciprocal**
   Friendships should be a two-way street. If you're always the one giving, it's time to evaluate whether the friendship is truly reciprocal. Ask yourself: Is this friendship based on mutual support and care, or is it one-sided? If it's the latter, it may be time to have an honest conversation about the state of the friendship, or in some cases, to let it go.

5. **Learn to Say No Without Guilt**
   Being a good friend doesn't mean you have to say yes to everything. If you're feeling drained or overwhelmed, it's okay to say no. You don't have to pick up every phone call, be available 24/7, or agree to every favor. Boundaries are essential for maintaining your emotional well-being. You can say something like, "I care about you, but I'm feeling a bit

stretched thin right now. Can we talk later?" No guilt necessary.

6. **Make Time for Friendships That Uplift You**
   Not all friendships drain you. Some friendships fill you up, make you laugh, and leave you feeling recharged. These are the friendships you should prioritize. Make time for the people who uplift you, who listen as much as they talk, and who make you feel valued for who you are—not just what you can offer them. Friendships should bring joy and balance to your life, not just obligation.

7. **Let Go of Friendships That No Longer Serve You**
   Sometimes, the hardest thing to do is let go of a friendship that's no longer healthy. But girl, it's okay to outgrow friendships. If a friendship is consistently draining, toxic, or one-sided, it may be time to let it go. You don't have to hold onto friendships out of guilt or loyalty—especially if they're no longer serving you. Letting go of a friendship doesn't mean you don't care—it means you care enough about yourself to prioritize your well-being.

Bestie or Doormat?

Curious to know if you've been balancing your friendships or if you've been doing all the heavy lifting? Take this quiz to find out!

1. When a friend calls you to vent about their problems, do you:
   - A. Listen, but make sure to share your own feelings when it's your turn.
   - B. Listen for hours and never get a word in about your own struggles.

3. How often do you feel drained after spending time with certain friends?
    - A. Rarely—I make time for friends who uplift me.
    - B. Often—I feel like I'm constantly giving without getting much in return.

5. When you need support, do you feel comfortable reaching out to your friends?
    - A. Yes, my friends are always there for me when I need them.
    - B. No, I don't want to burden them with my problems.

7. Do you have clear boundaries with your friends about your time and energy?
    - A. Yes, I set boundaries and don't feel guilty about them.
    - B. No, I often feel obligated to always be available.

Your Reflection

- **Mostly A's:** *Girl, you're doing YOU!* You've found a great balance in your friendships, where you're supportive but also prioritize your own needs. Keep nurturing those healthy, reciprocal friendships!
- **Mostly B's:** *Girl, it's time to reclaim your space.* You've been giving too much in your friendships and not getting enough in return. Start setting boundaries, communicating your needs, and remember—you deserve friendships that lift you up!

Chapter 9: Time – Guarding Your Calendar and Your Sanity

"Your identity is yours to define—embrace who you are, grow unapologetically, and let no one box you in."

Time—it's one of the most valuable resources we have, yet so many women give it away freely. Whether it's saying yes to extra work tasks, squeezing in last-minute favors for friends, or spending hours on obligations that don't really serve us, we find ourselves stretched thin. The result? We're constantly feeling rushed, overwhelmed, and wondering why there aren't enough hours in the day.

Girl, here's the hard truth: you're not getting any more time. You've got 24 hours in a day, just like everyone else, and how you use that time is up to you. The problem is, many of us don't guard our time like we should. We give it away to others, often out of guilt, obligation, or the fear of disappointing people. We sacrifice our time for things that aren't aligned with our goals, our well-being, or our happiness.

Here's the deal: your time is precious, and it's time to start treating it that way. You don't have to say yes to every request, and you don't have to feel bad for protecting your calendar. In fact, saying no and setting boundaries around your time is one of the most powerful acts of self-care you can do. When you start guarding your time, you make space for the things that truly matter—whether it's pursuing your passions, resting, or simply being present in your own life.

In this chapter, we're going to talk about how to reclaim your time and set boundaries around your schedule. We'll explore how to say no without guilt, how to stop overcommitting, and how to create a life where your calendar reflects your priorities—not someone else's. Because, girl, your time is too valuable to waste.

Let me introduce you to Rachel. Rachel is the queen of overcommitting. She's got a full-time job, volunteers at her kids' school, helps organize community events, and somehow finds herself saying yes to every social invitation that comes her way. Need someone to bake cookies for the fundraiser? Call Rachel. Want to plan a surprise party for a friend? Rachel's on it.

But here's the problem: Rachel is exhausted. She's running from one obligation to the next, barely catching her breath, and wondering when she'll ever have time for herself. Every Sunday night, she looks at her calendar for the upcoming week and groans, "Girl, how did I get myself into this again?"

One day, after staying up until midnight finishing yet another project she didn't really want to do, Rachel had a realization. "Girl, it's time to start saying no." She realized that her calendar was filled with things that weren't bringing her joy, weren't aligned with her goals, and were slowly burning her out. So, she made a bold decision—she started clearing her schedule and only saying yes to things that truly mattered.

Practical Tips and Strategies

If you've ever felt like Rachel—constantly overcommitting and struggling to find time for yourself—it's time to take back control of your calendar. Here's how to set boundaries around your time and protect your schedule like the precious resource it is:

1. **Learn the Power of No**
   The most powerful word in your time-management toolkit? No. It's time to start saying no to things that don't align with your priorities. This doesn't mean you're being rude or unhelpful—it means you're protecting your time and energy. The next time someone asks you to take on an extra task, think about whether it fits with your goals or if it's just going to add more stress. You can say something like, "I'd love to help, but my plate is full right now." Practice saying no with confidence and without guilt.

2. **Create a "Non-Negotiables" List**
   One of the best ways to reclaim your time is to create a list of non-negotiables—activities or moments in your day that you *will not* sacrifice. Maybe it's your morning workout, your weekly date night, or simply 30 minutes of quiet time before bed. Whatever your non-negotiables are, protect them fiercely. Block them out on your calendar, and don't let anything take their place. These are the things that keep you grounded, energized, and happy, so make sure they're prioritized.

3. **Assess Your Commitments**
   Take a hard look at your current commitments—both personal and professional. Are there things on your calendar that are draining you or don't align with your goals? If so, it's time to start letting go. You don't have to be everything to everyone, and you certainly don't have to say yes to things that don't bring value to your life. Start trimming the fat from your schedule and only keep the commitments that truly matter.

4. **Set Boundaries Around Work Time**
   For many women, work tasks have a way of spilling over into personal time. Whether it's answering emails after hours, staying late to finish projects, or taking work calls during your free time, it's easy to let work dominate your schedule. It's time to set clear boundaries. Let your colleagues and boss know when you're available and when you're off the clock. Stick to those boundaries, and don't feel guilty about it. Your personal time is just as important as your work time—if not more.

5. **Delegate and Outsource**
   You don't have to do everything yourself. If you're feeling overwhelmed by your to-do list, it's time to delegate. At work, delegate tasks to your team or ask for help from a colleague. At home, outsource what you can—whether that's hiring a

cleaning service, using grocery delivery, or enlisting your family members to help with chores. Freeing up your time doesn't make you lazy—it makes you smart.

6. **Use Time Blocks to Organize Your Day**

   One of the best ways to manage your time is by using time blocks. Instead of trying to multitask or juggle several things at once, dedicate specific blocks of time to certain tasks. For example, you might block out two hours in the morning for focused work, an hour in the afternoon for meetings, and 30 minutes in the evening for self-care. Time blocking helps you stay focused, prevents burnout, and ensures that your day is organized around your priorities.

7. **Protect Your Downtime**

   Downtime is not optional—it's essential. You need time to rest, recharge, and just be. Whether it's reading a book, taking a walk, or simply watching your favorite show, make sure you're carving out time in your schedule for relaxation. And when that time comes, protect it. Don't let work, errands, or other obligations encroach on your downtime. Your mental and emotional well-being depend on it.

8. **Regularly Review and Adjust Your Schedule**

   Life changes, and so do your priorities. Make it a habit to regularly review your calendar and adjust it as needed. If something no longer serves you, let it go. If new opportunities arise, make sure they fit with your existing commitments before saying yes. By regularly checking in with your schedule, you can ensure that it's always aligned with your goals and values.

Time Boss or Overcommitted Queen?

Wondering if you're the master of your schedule or if your calendar is running the show? Take this quiz and find out!

1. When someone asks you to take on an extra task or attend an event, do you:
   - A. Check your schedule and only say yes if it fits with your priorities.
   - B. Say yes automatically, even if it means overcommitting yourself.
3. How often do you block out time for yourself in your calendar?
   - A. Often—I make sure to prioritize my personal time.
   - B. Rarely—I usually fill my schedule with other obligations.
5. When you look at your calendar for the week, do you feel:
   - A. Calm and in control—I've got a good balance of work and personal time.
   - B. Overwhelmed—I've committed to too many things.
7. How easy is it for you to say no when someone asks for your time?
   - A. Easy—I'm comfortable setting boundaries around my time.
   - B. Difficult—I usually say yes, even when I don't want to.

How You Measure Up

- **Mostly A's:** *Girl, you're doing YOU!* You've got your time management down to a science, and you know how to guard your calendar and prioritize what matters. Keep owning your time and saying no to the things that don't serve you!

- **Mostly B's:** *Girl, it's time to reclaim your time.* You've been overcommitting yourself, and it's taking a toll. Start saying no, set some boundaries, and make sure your calendar reflects *your* priorities—not everyone else's.

Chapter 10: Identity – Reclaiming Who You Are at Every Stage of Life

> "Shine boldly, live authentically, and never shrink to fit someone else's narrative—this is your time to thrive."

Let's talk about identity—the core of who you are. Over the course of your life, your identity has likely gone through a number of changes. Maybe you've taken on roles like partner, mother, employee, boss, friend—but in the midst of all that, girl, have you ever paused and asked yourself, *Who am I really?* Who are you beyond the labels and roles society has placed on you? When you strip away the titles and the expectations, what's left?

For so many women, identity gets tied up in what they do for others or the roles they play in different areas of life. It's easy to become "so-and-so's mom," "the reliable employee," or "the supportive partner." And while those roles can be important parts of who you are, they shouldn't be *all* of who you are. If you're not careful, you can end up losing sight of your own wants, needs, and desires, and eventually, you might feel like you don't even recognize the woman staring back at you in the mirror.

But girl, here's the truth: your identity is yours to shape, define, and reclaim at every stage of your life. You're not stuck in any one version of yourself, and you don't have to let others' expectations define you. Whether you're going through a big life transition, starting a new chapter, or simply feeling disconnected from who you are, it's time to reconnect with *you* .

In this chapter, we're going to dive into how women often lose themselves in the roles they play, how to reclaim your identity, and how to make sure you're living in alignment with your true self. Because girl, you're so much more than the roles you play—you're a whole, complex, and dynamic person with dreams, desires, and potential that deserve to be at the forefront.

Let me tell you about Emma. Emma is the ultimate multi-tasker. She's a wife, a mom of two, and a manager at her company. She's always juggling a million things at once—taking care of her kids, keeping her relationship strong, and making sure everything runs smoothly at work. To everyone around her, Emma seems like she's got it all together. But deep down? Emma feels lost.

One day, after a particularly long week of taking care of everyone else, Emma sat down and realized she didn't even know what *she* wanted anymore. All of her energy had gone into being what everyone else needed—she was "Mom," "Wife," and "Manager," but she couldn't remember the last time she'd just been *Emma*. She missed her old hobbies, her passions, and the woman she used to be before life got so busy.

As she stared at her to-do list, Emma thought, "Girl, where did you go?" She realized that somewhere along the way, she had lost herself in the roles she was playing for everyone else. It was time to reconnect with who she truly was—and to make space for the things that mattered to her, not just the things that mattered to everyone else.

Practical Tips and Strategies

If you've ever felt like Emma—unsure of who you are beyond the roles you play—it's time to reclaim your identity. Here's how to reconnect with your true self and start living in alignment with who you really are:

1. **Get Clear on What Makes You *You***
   The first step to reclaiming your identity is taking a step back and reflecting on what truly makes you *you*. What are the things you love? What are your passions, your values, your dreams? Take some time to journal or reflect on the things that light you up—things that have nothing to do with the roles you play for others. Maybe it's a hobby you've neglected, a passion project you've put on hold, or a part of yourself that you haven't explored in a while. The goal is to reconnect with the core of who you are, outside of your responsibilities.

2. **Let Go of Other People's Expectations**
   One of the biggest reasons women lose their sense of identity is

because they're constantly trying to meet other people's expectations. Whether it's society's standards, family pressures, or even internalized beliefs about who you "should" be, these expectations can keep you from fully expressing yourself. It's time to let go of those expectations. You don't have to be perfect, and you don't have to fit into any mold. Start living for *you*, not for what others expect of you.

3. **Make Time for Self-Discovery**
Self-discovery doesn't stop after your teenage years, girl—it's a lifelong journey. Whether you're starting a new chapter in life, going through a transition, or just feeling disconnected, it's important to carve out time for self-discovery. This could be as simple as setting aside time each week for something you're passionate about, trying new things, or investing in your personal growth. The more time you spend exploring what makes you happy and fulfilled, the more connected you'll feel to your true self.

4. **Stop Defining Yourself by Your Roles**
While the roles you play—mother, partner, professional—are important, they shouldn't define your entire identity. You are so much more than the hats you wear. Start seeing yourself as a whole person, not just through the lens of the roles you play. You are an individual with your own desires, dreams, and strengths. When you stop defining yourself solely by your roles, you create space for growth, change, and self-expression.

5. **Reclaim Your Hobbies and Passions**
One of the first things to go when we're caught up in life's demands is our hobbies and passions. But girl, those are the things that keep you connected to who you are! Whether it's painting, reading, hiking, or cooking, make time for the things you love. Even if it's just 30 minutes a week, prioritizing your

hobbies is a powerful way to reconnect with yourself. Don't let life's responsibilities push your passions to the side.

6. **Embrace Change and Growth**

    Your identity is not fixed—it's constantly evolving as you grow and change. Sometimes we hold onto old versions of ourselves because they feel safe or familiar, but growth requires us to let go of who we used to be to make room for who we're becoming. Embrace the changes in your life and allow your identity to evolve with them. Don't be afraid to reinvent yourself, try new things, or pursue new dreams.

7. **Honor Your Boundaries**

    Part of reclaiming your identity is honoring the boundaries that protect your time, energy, and well-being. If you're constantly giving to others without taking time for yourself, it's easy to lose sight of who you are. Set boundaries that allow you to prioritize your self-care, your passions, and your personal growth. Remember, girl, you are worthy of the time and space to just *be* .

True to You or Playing a Role?

Curious to know if you're living in alignment with your true self or if you've been shrinking into the roles others expect you to play? Take this quiz to find out!

1. When you think about who you are, do you:
    - A. Feel connected to your passions and values.
    - B. Mostly think about the roles you play for others (mom, wife, employee, etc.).

3. How often do you make time for your hobbies or passions?
    - A. Regularly—I prioritize doing things that make me happy.
    - B. Rarely—life's demands keep me too busy.
5. Do you feel like you're living for yourself or for other people's expectations?
    - A. I live for myself and follow my own path.
    - B. I often feel like I'm trying to meet others' expectations.
7. How comfortable are you with embracing change and growth in your identity?
    - A. Very comfortable—I see growth as part of the journey.
    - B. Not very comfortable—I tend to hold onto old versions of myself.

The Big Reveal

- **Mostly A's:** *Girl, you're doing YOU!* You're living in alignment with your true self, embracing change, and prioritizing what makes you happy. Keep honoring your identity and following your path!
- **Mostly B's:** *Girl, it's time to reclaim your identity.* You've been living for others for too long, and it's time to reconnect with who *you* are. Start prioritizing your passions, letting go of expectations, and living in alignment with your true self.

Conclusion: Girl, You've Got This!

> "Your journey is yours alone—walk it with purpose, set your boundaries boldly, and never forget that you deserve the space to grow, thrive, and shine."

You've made it to the end of *Girl Please, Do You!* —and what a journey it's been! We've talked about all the ways women shrink themselves in life—whether it's in relationships, careers, friendships, or even in how we manage our time and money. But now, after going through this book, you've learned the truth: you don't have to play small, you don't have to meet everyone else's expectations, and you absolutely *don't* have to sacrifice yourself for the sake of others.

In every chapter, we explored different areas of life where you might be shrinking, and we uncovered the tools to break free and start living boldly, authentically, and unapologetically. You've seen how setting boundaries isn't about pushing people away—it's about protecting your peace and creating space for the things that really matter. You've learned that self-care isn't selfish; it's necessary for you to thrive and show up as the best version of yourself.

But here's the thing: this journey doesn't end here. The lessons you've learned throughout this book are meant to be applied every day. Life will always have its challenges, and there will always be pressures to conform, to shrink, to bend to others' expectations. But girl, you've got the tools to handle those challenges now. You've learned how to say no, how to protect your time, how to speak up for yourself, and how to prioritize your own well-being.

This conclusion is not the closing of a chapter—it's the beginning of a new way of living. A life where you put yourself first, without guilt. A life where you stop shrinking and start shining. So let's take a moment to summarize the key messages you'll be carrying forward into the rest of your life.

Key Takeaways from *Girl Please, Do You!*

1. **Boundaries Are Your Best Friend**
   At the core of every chapter, we talked about boundaries—whether it was setting them in your relationships, your friendships, or even with yourself. Boundaries are what protect your energy, your time, and your well-being. They let people know where you stand and what you're willing to tolerate. But

more importantly, boundaries are what give you the freedom to live life on your terms.

Going forward, remember that boundaries are not just a one-time thing—they need to be revisited and adjusted as you grow and change. The boundaries that worked for you last year might need to shift as you evolve. Don't be afraid to set new boundaries when necessary, and don't feel guilty about enforcing them. You are allowed to protect your peace, girl!

1. **Self-Care Is Non-Negotiable**

   We've talked a lot about how women often sacrifice their health, well-being, and personal time to take care of others. But what we've uncovered is that self-care is not optional—it's essential. You cannot pour from an empty cup, and if you're not taking care of yourself, you won't be able to show up fully for the people you love.

Going forward, make self-care a regular part of your routine. This doesn't mean just bubble baths and spa days (although those are great). Self-care can be as simple as saying no to something that drains you, taking a walk to clear your mind, or carving out time to pursue your passions. The key is to prioritize your well-being every single day, without guilt.

1. **You Are More Than Your Roles**

   One of the most powerful lessons from this book is that you are not defined by the roles you play. Whether you're a mother, partner, employee, or friend, those roles are just parts of who you are—they don't define your entire identity. It's easy to lose yourself in these roles, but girl, you are so much more than the hats you wear for other people.

Going forward, make sure you're honoring the person *behind* the roles. Take time to reconnect with who you are at your core—your passions, your dreams, and your desires. Don't let the expectations of others dictate how you live your life. You are allowed to evolve, to change, and to grow into the fullest version of yourself.

1. **Saying No Is a Superpower**
   Throughout this book, we've explored the power of saying no—and let's be real, it's not always easy. But learning how to say no is one of the most liberating skills you can develop. When you say no to things that don't serve you, you're making room for the things that truly matter.

Going forward, don't be afraid to use your "no" when needed. Whether it's turning down a social event you don't have the energy for, declining an extra task at work, or simply protecting your downtime, saying no allows you to reclaim your time and energy. And remember, saying no doesn't make you a bad person—it makes you someone who values herself.

1. **Fear Isn't the Enemy—Inaction Is**
   We talked about how fear can hold us back, keep us playing small, and prevent us from chasing our dreams. But here's the truth: fear is a normal part of life. Everyone feels fear, but the key is not letting it stop you from taking action. Fear isn't the enemy—inaction is.

Going forward, recognize that fear will always be there in some form, but it doesn't have to control you. Every time you push through fear and take a step toward your goals, you build courage. And the more you do it, the easier it becomes. Don't let fear keep you stuck, girl—feel the fear, and do it anyway.

1. **Your Time Is Yours to Guard**
   One of the most valuable lessons in this book is that your time is your most precious resource, and you don't have to give it away freely. You've learned how to set boundaries around your

schedule, how to stop overcommitting, and how to say no to things that don't align with your priorities.

Going forward, guard your time like it's gold—because it is. Only say yes to things that bring value, joy, or growth into your life. And don't feel guilty for declining things that drain your energy. Your time is yours to manage, and no one else has the right to tell you how to spend it.

Keep Applying These Lessons to Your Life

The lessons in this book aren't just concepts—they're tools for real life. And girl, I know life can get messy, busy, and overwhelming. There will be days when it feels easier to slip back into old habits—overcommitting, people-pleasing, shrinking yourself to meet others' expectations. But every time you catch yourself doing it, remember the tools you've learned here.

When you're faced with a decision, ask yourself:

- Am I saying yes because I want to or because I feel obligated?
- Does this serve my well-being, my goals, or my happiness?
- Am I shrinking myself to make someone else comfortable?

By asking yourself these questions, you can keep yourself on track, living authentically and in alignment with your true desires. You've come too far to go back to a life where you put everyone else's needs ahead of your own. This is your time, girl, and you deserve to live fully and freely.

Embrace the Journey

As you continue applying these lessons to your life, remember that this is a journey—there's no final destination where you'll have it all figured out. There will be ups and downs, challenges, and triumphs. But that's the beauty of it. Every step you take toward reclaiming your boundaries, your time, and your identity is a step toward a more fulfilling, empowered life.

Don't be afraid to make mistakes along the way. Don't be afraid to adjust your boundaries, shift your priorities, or reinvent yourself when needed. Life is constantly changing, and you have the power to adapt and grow with it. Embrace the journey, knowing that you're equipped with everything you need to live boldly and authentically.

Girl, Keep Shining!

As we wrap up, I want to leave you with one final thought: *You are enough, exactly as you are.* You don't have to shrink, conform, or dim your light to make others comfortable. You are worthy of taking up space, of setting boundaries, and of living a life that brings you joy.

So, girl, keep shining. Keep setting those boundaries. Keep saying no to the things that don't serve you and yes to the things that make your soul come alive. You are powerful, capable, and deserving of all the good things life has to offer.

This is your time to thrive—not just survive. To live boldly, unapologetically, and fully as yourself. Remember, the world needs more women who are unapologetically themselves—women who are living out loud, taking up space, and embracing their power. And girl, that's you.

Go out there and do YOU, because no one else can do it better.